In Search of Small Gods

Also by Jim Harrison

JIM HARRISON

In Search of Small Gods

Copper Canyon Press

Port Townsend, Washington

Copyright 2009 by Jim Harrison

All rights reserved

Printed in the United States of America

Cover art: Russell Chatham, *Spring Moonrise over the Sangre de Cristo Mountains,*
from the "Colorado Suite," 2000. Lithograph, 45″ × 34″.

Copper Canyon Press is in residence at Fort Worden State Park in Port Townsend,
Washington, under the auspices of Centrum. Centrum is a gathering place for
artists and creative thinkers from around the world, students of all ages and
backgrounds, and audiences seeking extraordinary cultural enrichment.

LIBRARY OF CONGRESS CATALOGING-IN-PUBLICATION DATA

Harrison, Jim, 1937–
In search of small gods / Jim Harrison.
p. cm.
Poems.
ISBN 978-1-55659-300-0 (cloth: alk. paper)
I. Title.
PS3558.A6716 2009
811′.54 – dc22
2008039992

3 5 7 9 8 6 4 2

FIRST PRINTING

COPPER CANYON PRESS
Post Office Box 271
Port Townsend, Washington 98368

www.coppercanyonpress.org

to
Ted and Dan

Walker, your footsteps
are the road, and nothing more.
Walker, there is no road,
the road is made by walking.
Walking you make the road,
and turning to look behind
you see the path you never
again will step upon.
Walker, there is no road,
only foam trails on the sea.

※

Caminante, son tus huellas
el camino, y nada más;
caminante, no hay camino,
se hace camino al andar.
Al andar se hace camino,
y al volver la vista atrás
se ve la senda que nunca
se ha de volver a pisar.
Caminante, no hay camino,
sino estelas en la mar.

ANTONIO MACHADO, "Proverbs and Songs #29,"
translated by Willis Barnstone

ACKNOWLEDGMENTS

Poems from *In Search of Small Gods* appeared in the following publications, sometimes in slightly different form:

The Best American Poetry 2009: "Sunday Discordancies"

Brick: "Larson's Holstein Bull," "Barking," "Eleven Dawns with Su Tung-p'o"

Conjunctions: "Larson's Holstein Bull," "Hard Times," "Easter 2008"

Earth First! Journal: "Alien"

Five Points: "Sunday Discordancies," "Fibber," "Early Fishing," "Mapman," "My Leader," "On Horseback in China"

The House of Your Dream: An International Collection of Prose Poetry: "My Leader," "Very Small Wars"

Narrative: "Land Divers," "Burning the Ditches"

Orion: "New World"

Playboy: "The World's Fastest White Woman"

Poetry: "Barking"

TriQuarterly: "I Believe"

Virginia Quarterly Review: "The Golden Window"

The Writer's Almanac: "The Quarter"

Contents

❈

In Search of Small Gods

I Believe

I believe in steep drop-offs, the thunderstorm across the lake
in 1949, cold winds, empty swimming pools,
the overgrown path to the creek, raw garlic,
used tires, taverns, saloons, bars, gallons of red wine,
abandoned farmhouses, stunted lilac groves,
gravel roads that end, brush piles, thickets, girls
who haven't quite gone totally wild, river eddies,
leaky wooden boats, the smell of used engine oil,
turbulent rivers, lakes without cottages lost in the woods,
the primrose growing out of a cow skull, the thousands
of birds I've talked to all of my life, the dogs
that talked back, the Chihuahuan ravens that follow
me on long walks. The rattler escaping the cold hose,
the fluttering unknown gods that I nearly see
from the left corner of my blind eye, struggling
to stay alive in a world that grinds them underfoot.

Calendars

Back in the blue chair in front of the green studio
another year has passed, or so they say, but calendars lie.
They're a kind of cosmic business machine like
their cousin clocks but break down at inopportune times.
Fifty years ago I learned to jump off the calendar
but I kept getting drawn back on for reasons
of greed and my imperishable stupidity.
Of late I've escaped those fatal squares
with their razor-sharp numbers for longer and longer.
I had to become the moving water I already am,
falling back into the human shape in order
not to frighten my children, grandchildren, dogs and friends.
Our old cat doesn't care. He laps the water where my face used to be.

Larson's Holstein Bull

Death waits inside us for a door to open.
Death is patient as a dead cat.
Death is a doorknob made of flesh.
Death is that angelic farm girl
gored by the bull on her way home
from school, crossing the pasture
for a shortcut. In the seventh grade
she couldn't read or write. She wasn't a virgin.
She was "simpleminded," we all said.
It was May, a time of lilacs and shooting stars.
She's lived in my memory for sixty years.
Death steals everything except our stories.

New Moon

Why does the new moon give anyone hope?
Nevertheless it does and always has for me
and likely does for that Mexican poet with no pesos,
maybe a couple of tortillas, chewing them while sitting
on a smooth rock beside a creek in the Sierra Madres
seeing the new moon tilted delicately away from Venus,
the faint silver light, the ever-so-small sliver
of white enamel rippling in the creek, the same moon,
he thinks, that soothed the Virgin in her great doubt
over the swollen belly beneath her breasts.
The fatherless son had two new moons in his forty days
in the wilderness, the second one telling him it was time
to become God and enter the beast of history.
This poet, though, ignores the sacraments of destiny
and only wants a poem to sing the liquid gift of night.

Tomorrow

I'm hoping to be astonished tomorrow
by I don't know what:
not the usual undiscovered bird in the cold
snowy willows, garishly green and yellow,
and not my usual death, which I've done
before with Borodin's music
used in *Kismet,* and angels singing
"Stranger in Paradise," that sort of thing,
and not the thousand naked women
running a marathon in circles around me
while I swivel on a writerly chair
keeping an eye on my favorites.
What could it be, this astonishment,
but falling into a liquid mirror
to finally understand that the purpose
of earth is earth? It's plain as night.
She's willing to sleep with us a little while.

Hard Times

The other boot doesn't drop from heaven.
I've made this path and nobody else
leading crookedly up through the pasture
where I'll never reach the top of Antelope Butte.
It is here where my mind begins to learn
my heart's language on this endless
wobbly path, veering south and north
informed by my all-too-vivid dreams
which are a compass without a needle.
Today the gods speak in drunk talk
pulling at a heart too old for this walk,
a cold windy day kneeling at the mouth
of the snake den where they killed 800 rattlers.
Moving higher my thumping chest recites the names
of a dozen friends who have died in recent years,
names now incomprehensible as the mountains
across the river far behind me.
I'll always be walking up toward Antelope Butte.
Perhaps when we die our names are taken
from us by a divine magnet and are free
to flutter here and there within the bodies
of birds. I'll be a simple crow
who can reach the top of Antelope Butte.

Age Sixty-nine

I keep waiting without knowing
what I'm waiting for.
I saw the setting moon at dawn
roll over the mountain
and perhaps into the dragon's mouth
until tomorrow evening.

There is this circle I walk
that I have learned to love.
I hope one day to be a spiral
but to the birds I'm a circle.

A thousand Spaniards died looking
for gold in a swamp when it was
in the mountains in clear sight beyond.

Here, though, on local earth my heart
is at rest as a groundling, letting
my mind take flight as it will,
no longer waiting for good or bad news.

Often, lately, the night is a cold maw
and stars the scattered white teeth of the gods,
which spare none of us. At dawn I have birds,
clearly divine messengers that I don't understand
yet day by day feel the grace of their intentions.

Sunday Discordancies

This morning I seem to hear the nearly inaudible
whining grind of creation similar to the harmonics
of pine trees in the wind. My outrageously lovely
hollyhocks are now collapsing of their own weight,
clearly too big for their britches. I'm making notes
for a novel called *The End of Man, and Not Incidentally,*
Women and Children, a fable for our low-living time.
Quite early after walking the dogs, who are frightened
of the sandhill cranes in the pasture, I fried some ham
with a fresh peach, a touch of brown sugar and clove.
Pretty good but I was wondering at how the dogs
often pretend the sandhill cranes don't exist despite
their mighty squawks, the way we can't hear
the crying of coal miners and our wounded in Iraq.
A friend on his deathbed cried and said it felt good.
He was crying because he couldn't eat, a lifelong habit.
My little grandson Silas cried painfully until he was fed
macaroni and cheese and then he was merry indeed.
I'm not up to crying this morning over that pretty girl
in the rowboat fifty-five years ago. I heard on the radio
that we creatures have about a billion and a half
heartbeats to use. Voles and birds use theirs fast
as do meth heads and stockbrokers, while whales
and elephants are slower. This morning I'm thinking
of recounting mine to see exactly where I am.
I warn the hummingbirds out front, "Just slow down,"
as they chase me away from the falling hollyhocks.

Hospital

No poems about copious blood in the urine,
tumors as big as a chicken beneath the waistline.
We've long since found these truths quite evident.
Life has never been in remission or rehabilitation.
Life doesn't sing those homely words we invented
to blind our eyes to this idyll of metamorphoses
which can include unbearable pain and unbearable joy.
Death by starvation or gluttony are but a block away
in some cities known to us for their artifacts.
Today I regretted closing this lowly stinkbug in the gate,
feeling the crunch of it beneath my foot to push it on.
My heart must open to the cosmos with no language
unless we invent it moment by moment in order to breathe.
A girl in a green bathing suit swam across the green river
above which swallows flocked in dark whirls.
She swam toward a green bank lined with green willows.
The guiding light of our sun averages half a day.

Child Fear

Sour milk. Rotten eggs. Bumblebees.
Giant women. Falling through the privy hole.
The snake under the dock that bit my foot.
Snapping turtles. Electric fences. Howling bears.
The neighbor's big dog that tore apart
the black lamb. Oil wells. Train wheels.
Dentists and doctors. Hitler and Tōjō. Eye pain.
School superintendent with three gold teeth.
Cow's infected udder, angry draft horse.
School fire. Snake under hay bale. Life's end.

That your dead dogs won't meet you in heaven.

Another Old Mariachi

His voice cracks on tremolo notes.
He recalls the labia of women
as the undersides of dove wings,
the birds he retrieved as a boy for rich hunters.
Now in a cantina outside of Hermosillo
he thinks, I don't have much life left
but I have my songs. I'm still the child
with sand sticking to my dew-wet feet
going to the fountain for morning water.

Spring

This small liquid mouth in the forest
is called a spring, but it is really
a liquid mouth that keeps all of the secrets
of what has happened here, speaking in the unparsed
language of water, how the sky was once closer
and a fragment of a burned-out star boiled its water.
This liquid mouth has been here since the glaciers
and has seen a few creatures die with its billions
of moving eyes–an ancient bear going bald who went to sleep
and never knew that it died, and an indian woman
who plunged in her fevered face, deciding to breathe
the water. Since it is a god there is a delight
in becoming unfrozen in spring, to see the coyote
jump five feet into the air to catch a lowly mouse,
or to reflect a hundred thousand bright moons,
to sleep under a deep mantle of snow or feel
the noses of so many creatures who came to drink,
even the man who sits on the forest floor, enjoying
the purity of this language he hopes to learn someday.

Manuela

When I left Seville I wanted to write
a poem as large as the soul of Manuela,
but no book could contain her. You need a country,
Spain, the sun-gristled murderer of poets.

On the train to Granada I read a newspaper
that said children in Somalia were eating
their own lips in desperation, gulping the air
as if the sky herself was something to eat.
The train slowed in the middle of a ranch
of fighting bulls, bulls as mean as the world.

Several gods walking south through Somalia
saw the black tinkertoy children and decided
to leave the earth after being here before
Helen's face sank so many ships.

Manuela dances the eyes of the children,
a moon without golf clubs, the muddy Guadalquivir,
her fear and love of the bull of the earth.

Back when I was young and still alive
there were almost too many gods. You could see
them ripple in the water before the lake's ice
melted in April, the loons and curlews giving them voice.

Cow Meditation

Whenever I'm on the verge of a book tour I begin to think
of Guadalajara. This has been going on for decades.
On tote boards in airports in Chicago and Dallas
and Los Angeles you see Guadalajara listed, so far away
from signing books in Salt Lake and Denver, and from here
at Hard Luck Ranch near the Mexican border
where they're loading cattle for market on a cold,
rainy day with distant Guadalajara a new kind of moon.
Sleet is melting on the back of a baloney bull. He broke
his dick somehow and is destined to be lunch meat.
Twelve cattle are near the end of their lives without knowing it,
ten quite old and two young and scrawny with illness.
In this rough country no one survives with bad teeth.
A rare Aztec thrush visits the pyracantha tree
two feet from my window, looking for a mate.
Last year it was a male waiting for a female to show up.
Life is an honor, albeit anonymously delivered.
Before Rancher Bob leaves for market he tells me
that a cow as old as a sixty-five-year-old woman escaped
by jumping three six-foot-high corral fences and running
up a canyon back into the mountains. "She's too smart
to be caught again," he says. When my plate is too full
I think, Clean the plate by flying to Guadalajara.

Prayer

Are all of these wrongful prayers gumming
up the skies like smog over Los Angeles?
We never stop making a special case for ourselves.
May the Coyotes kill the Lobos in the Regional Finals.
The lottery would be nice. Bring my dead child back to life.
May the weather clear for the church picnic on Saturday.
Let Christina be my true love not Bob's or Ralph's.
May we destroy all terrorist countries except the children.
In France the sun through stained-glass windows
quilted the sanctuary with the faint rose light of Jesus' blood.
10,000 different asses, clutched in fear, sat on these pews.
Perhaps planes fly holes in all our stalled prayers,
and birds migrate through them as they rise up
or down toward the ninety billion galaxies we know of,
those seeds of the gods in this endlessly flowering universe.
As a child I prayed in my hiding place beneath the roots
of an overturned tree that the sight would return to my blind eye.
The sight is only enough to see the moon,
the rising sun, the blur of stars.

Lunar

Out in the nighttime in the caliche-gravel driveway
doing a shuffle dance to the music of the lunar eclipse,
a dark gray and reddish smear blocking the moon.
I'm embarrassed by my dance steps learned
from the Ojibwe over fifty years ago,
but then who's watching but a few startled birds,
especially a canyon wren nesting in a crack of the huge
rock face? Without the moon's white light the sky
is suddenly overpopulated with stars like China and India
with people. The stars cast the longest of shadows.
I dance until I'm a breathless old fool thinking
that the spirit of this blinded moon is as real
as that enormous toad that used to bury itself
between the house and the barn of our farm
in Lake Leelanau. One evening I watched him slowly
erupt from the ground. Now the moon's white light
begins to show itself, shining off looming Red Mountain
where years ago I'm told a Mexican boy climbed
to the top to play a song more closely to his dead sister.
Luna, luna, luna, we must sing to praise living and dead.

Singer

My dream of becoming a Mexican singer
is drifting away.
It reminds me of the etching on my journal
of a naked girl
grasping the cusp of the moon with
both hands.
She's surrounded by stars. No one is strong enough
to hold the moon for long.
I simply wanted my musical sobs to drift
on the airways
to a larger audience with songs about
hearts and pistols,
the curious nonresistance of our human
flesh to bullets,
the love my eye developed in the doctor's office
for a girl
fifty years younger than me. And sadder
songs about the dogs
that ate the child in Tucson, or the twelve-year-
old virgin girl
falling before the red hammer of the lout who
loved to lick tears,
the boy who stabbed his own heart on flunking
the rigors of geometry,
the relentless yips of the coyotes chasing
a deer last night.
What can I make of this world of details
that doesn't yield
to literature, that doesn't feel quite right

enclosed in a slender book?
The indian boy born without a tongue
is a soup eater,
and the fourteen-year-old girl in Iraq has her teeth frozen
together in rape.
In the night of our age how can I translate
their unworded words?

Poor Girls

They're amputating the head of the poor girl
to put it on a rich girl who needs it to survive.
This is always happening to poor girls
who are without defense. They've sold the contents
of their hope chests on eBay. The never-worn
size 18 wedding dress is cheap because it's black.
I've watched poor girls in diners eat piles of cheap potatoes.
Of course they sometimes marry poor guys
who leave them to work in oil fields or join the army.
I know one who has four children and takes care
of her vegetable husband home from sunny Iraq
with the mental age of a baby in big diapers.
Unmarried poor girls often have bowling clubs
and drink lots of beer Tuesday nights at Starlight Lanes.
They know they're largely invisible cleaning motels:
receptionists, waitresses, fast-food cooks, nannies.
Still they're jolly with friends and nephews and nieces.
I see a great big one wearing a bright blue bathing suit
when I go trout fishing. She parks her old Plymouth
and floats on a truck inner tube on a mile of fast water,
gets out, wheels the tube back through a pasture, does it again.

Limb Dancers

Of course we're born in the long shadow
of our coffins or urns. So what can we do except
open ourselves wide to life herself
rather than the numbers game of time and money?
You'd best avoid the voyage to the bottom of the sea
from which most don't arise, or come up
only halfway, struggling for the light of childhood
before they named themselves Self, a temporary measure.
Back then you did not separate yourself very far
from birds or cows, though you failed all attempts
to fly, or moo with deep basso strength. Fishing
and dogs carried you through months of pain,
and also hard rain playing the tin-roof instrument.
The heart opened wider and wider and the skin grew
thinner and thinner until a few insignificant gods
who had lost their jobs in the city parks took up residence
in the forest behind our old house, then moved farther
on down here on the Mexican border where they joined
the Chihuahuan ravens along the creek, those noisy
limb dancers. When they wish they move inside each other.
We can find them by looking when we give up our skin.

Night Ride

The full moon dark orange from another forest
fire, and at four AM the massive sound of elephants
trumpeting in the yard and in Weber's sheep
pasture next door. Out the bedroom window I saw
the elephants big as shadowy dump trucks drifting
to and fro. Sat there at the window watching
until the elephants disappeared at first light
when nature became livid with its essence,
oceans of grass as blade-thin green snakes writhing,
birds flying in ten dimensions of Dürer perfection.
I then circled earth in a warm clear bubble,
remembering the black girl from another life
who became the Virgin Mary and gave me the gift
of seeing the white moon behind a thunderstorm
where she was washed as if by a waterfall,
gave me the gift of seeing these cows and sheep,
the bear near the garden, on all sides at once.
Here I was Jim the poet drifting the edges of night,
not sure he wished to be kidnapped by the gods.

The Golden Window

By accident my heart lifted with a rush.
Gone for weeks, finally home on a darkish day
of blustery wind, napped, waking in a few minutes
and the sun had come clean and crept around the house,
this light from one of trillions of stars
falling through the window skeined
by the willow's greenish bright yellow leaves
so that my half-asleep head opened wide
for the first time in many months, a cold sunstroke,
so yellow-gold, so gold-yellow, yellow-gold,
this eye beyond age bathed in yellow light.

❋

Seventy days on the river with a confusion between
river turbulence and human tribulation. We are here
to be curious not consoled. The gift of the gods
is consciousness not my forlorn bleating prayers
for equilibrium, the self dog-paddling in circles
on its own alga-lidded pond. Emily Walter wrote:
    "We are given rivers so we know our hearts
    can break, but still keep us breathing."

❋

When you run through the woods blindfolded
you're liable to collide with trees, I thought
one hot afternoon on the river. You can't drown yourself
if you swim well. We saw some plovers

and then a few yellowlegs with their peculiar cries,
and I remembered a very cold, windy September day
with Matthiessen and Danny when the birds lifted
me far out of myself. It was so cold and blustery the avian
world descended into the river valley and while fishing
we saw a golden eagle, two immature and two adult
bald eagles, two prairie falcons, two peregrines, Cooper's
hawks, two Swainson's, a sharp-shinned,
a rough-legged, a harrier, five turkey vultures,
three ospreys, and also saw buffleheads, wigeon,
teal, mallards, mourning doves, kingfishers,
ring-billed gulls, killdeer, spotted plovers,
sandpipers and sandhill cranes.
They also saw us. If a peregrine sees fifty times better
than we, what do we look like to them?
Unanswerable.

❈

Nearing seventy there is a tinge of the usually
unseen miraculous when you wake up alive
from a night's sleep or a nap. We always rise in the terrifying
posture of the living. Some days the river is incomprehensible.
No, not the posture, but that a terrifying beauty
is born within us. I think of the twenty-acre thicket
my mother planted after the deaths forty years ago,
the thicket now nearly impenetrable as its own beauty.
Across the small pond the green heron looked at me quizzically—
who is this? I said I wasn't sure at that moment
wondering if the green heron could be Mother.

❈

Now back in the Absarokas I'm awake
to these diffuse corridors of light. The grizzlies
have buried themselves below that light cast down
across the mountain meadow, following a canyon
to the valley floor where the rattlesnakes will also sleep
until mid-April. Meanwhile we'll travel toward the border
with the birds. The moon is swollen tonight
and the mountain this summer I saw bathed
in a thunderstorm now bathes itself in a mist of snow.

❋

Rushing, turbulent water and light, convinced by animals
and rivers that nature only leads us to herself,
so openly female through the window of my single eye.
For half a year my alphabet blinded me to beauty,
forgetting my nature which came from the boy lost
comfortably in the woods, how and why he suspected home,
this overmade world where old paths are submerged
in metal and cement.

❋

This morning in the first clear sunlight making its way
over the mountains, the earth covered with crunchy frost,
I walked the dogs past Weber's sheep pasture
where a ram was covering a ewe who continued eating,
a wise and experienced woman. I headed due west
up the slope toward Antelope Butte in the delicious
cold still air, turning at the irrigation ditch hearing
the staccato howl of sandhill cranes behind me,
a couple of hundred rising a mile away from Cargill's
alfalfa, floating up into the white mist rising
from the frost, and moving north in what I judge

is the wrong direction for this weather. Birds make mistakes,
so many dying against windows and phone wires.
I continued west toward the snake den to try to catch
the spirit of the place when it's asleep, the sheer otherness
of hundreds of rattlesnakes sleeping in a big ball
deep in the rocky earth beneath my feet. The dogs,
having been snake trained, are frightened of this place.
So am I. So much protective malevolence. I fled.
Back home in the studio, a man-made wonder. We planted
a chokecherry tree near the window and now through cream-
colored blinds the precise silhouette of the bare branches,
gently but firmly lifting my head, a Chinese screen
that no one made which I accept from the nature of light.

❋

I think of Mother's thicket as her bird garden.
How obsessed she was with these creatures. When I told
her a schizophrenic in Kentucky wrote, "Birds are holes
in heaven through which a man may pass," her eyes teared.
She lost husband and daughter to the violence of the road
and I see their spirits in the bird garden. On our last night
a few years ago she asked me, "Are we the same species as God?"
At eighty-five she was angry that the New Testament wasn't fair
to women and then she said, "During the Great Depression
we had plenty to eat," meaning at the farmhouse,
barn and chicken coop a hundred yards to the north
that are no longer there, disappeared with the inhabitants.
The child is also the mother of the man.

❋

In the U.P. in the vast place southeast of the river
I found my way home by following the path

where my shadow was the tallest
which led to the trail which led
to another trail which led to the road home
to the cabin where I wrote to her:
"Found two dead redtail hawks, missing
their breasts, doubtless a goshawk took them
as one nests just north of here a half mile
in a tall hemlock on the bend of the river."

❄

With only one eye I've learned
to celebrate vision, the eye a painter,
the eye a monstrous fleshy camera
which can't stop itself in the dark
where it sees its private imagination.
The tiny eye that sees the cosmos overhead.

❄

Last winter I lost heart between each of seven cities.
Planes never land with the same people who boarded.

❄

Walking Mary and Zilpha every morning I wonder
how many dogs are bound by regret
because they are captured by our imaginations
and affixed there by our need to have them do
as we wish when their hearts are quite otherwise.

❄

I hope to define my life, whatever is left,
by migrations, south and north with the birds
and far from the metallic fever of clocks,
the self staring at the clock saying, "I must do this."
I can't tell the time on the tongue of the river
in the cool morning air, the smell of the ferment
of greenery, the dust off the canyon's rock walls,
the swallows swooping above the scent of raw water.

*

Maybe we're not meant to wake up completely.
I'm trying to think of what I can't remember.
Last week in France I read that the Ainu in Japan
receive messages from the gods through willow trees,
so I'm not the only one. I looked down into the garden
of Matignon and wondered at the car trip the week before
where at twilight in Narbonne 27,000 blackbirds swirled,
and that night from the window
it was eerie with a slip of the waning moon
off the right shoulder of the Romanesque cathedral
with Venus sparkling shamelessly above the moon,
Venus over whom the church never had any power.
Who sees? Whose eye is this? A day later in Collioure
from the Hermitage among vineyards in the mountains
I could look down steep canyons still slightly green
from the oaks in November to the startling blue of the Mediterranean,
storm-wracked from the mistral's seventy-knot winds,
huge lumpy whitecaps, their crests looking toward Africa.

*

I always feared losing my remaining eye,
my singular window to the world. When closed it sees

the thousands of conscious photos I've taken with it,
impressionist rather than crystalline, from a lion's mouth
in the Serengeti in 1972 to a whale's eye in the Humboldt current,
to the mountain sun gorged with the color of forest
fires followed by a moon orange as a simple orange,
a thousand girls and women I've seen but never met,
the countless birds I adopted since losing the eye in 1945
including an albino grouse creamy as that goshawk's breast
that came within feet of Mother in our back pasture,
the female trogon that appeared when Dalva
decided to die, and the thousands of books out of whose print
vision is created in the mind's eye, as real as any garden at dawn.

❋

No rhapsodies today. Home from France
and the cold wind and a foot of snow have destroyed
my golden window, but then the memory
has always been more vivid than the life. The memory
is the not-quite-living museum of our lives.
Sometimes its doors are insufferably wide open
with black stars in a gray sky, and horses
clattering in and out, our dead animals resting here
and there but often willing to come to life again
to greet us, parents and brothers and sisters sitting
at the August table laughing while they eat twelve
fresh vegetables from the garden. Rivers, creeks, lakes
over which birds funnel like massive schools of minnows.
In memory the clocks have drowned themselves, leaving
time to the life spans of trees. The world of our lives
comes unbidden as night.

Advice

A ratty old man, an Ojibwe alcoholic who lived to be eighty-eight
and chewed Red Man tobacco as a joke, told me a few years back
that time lasted seven times longer than we "white folks" think. This
irritated me. We were sitting on the porch of his shack drinking a
bottle of Sapphire gin that I brought over. He liked expensive gin.
An old shabby-furred bear walked within ten feet of us on the way to
the bird feeder for a mouthful of sunflower seed. "That bear was a
pissant as a boy. He'd howl in my window until I made him popcorn
with bacon grease. You should buy a green Dodge from the fifties, a
fine car but whitewash it in the late fall, and scrub it off May 1. Never
drive the highways, take back roads. The Great Spirit made dirt not
cement and blacktop. On your walks in the backcountry get to where
you're going, then walk like a heron or sandhill crane. They don't
miss a thing. Study turtles and chickadees. These bears and wolves
around here have too much power for us to handle right. I used to
take naps near a female bear who farted a lot during blueberry sea-
son. Always curtsey to the police and they'll leave you alone. They
don't like to deal with what they can't figure out. Only screw fatter
women because they feed you better. This skinny woman over near
Munising gave me some crunchy cereal that cut my gums. A big-
ger woman will cook you ham and eggs. I've had my .22 Remington
seventy years and now it looks like it's made out of duct tape. Ker-
osene is your best fuel. If you row a boat you can't help but go in
a circle. Once I was so cold and hungry I ate a hot deer heart raw. I
felt its last beat in my mouth. Sleep outside as much as you can but
don't close your eyes. I had this pet garter snake that lived in my
coat pocket for three years. She would come out at night and eat the
flies in my shack. Think of your mind as a lake. Give away half the
money you make or you'll become a bad person. During nights of

big moons try walking as slow as a skunk. You'll like it. Don't ever go in a basement. Now I see Teddy's fish tug coming in. If you buy a six-pack I'll get us a big lake trout from Teddy. I got three bucks burning a hole in my pocket. Women like their feet rubbed. Bring them wildflowers. My mom died when I was nine years old. I got this idea she became a bird and that's why I talk to birds. Way back then I thought the Germans and Japs would kill the world but here we are about ready to cook a fish. What more could you want on an August afternoon?"

Fibber

My bird-watching friends tell me, "You're always seeing birds that
don't exist." And I answer that my eye seems to change nearly every-
thing it sees and is also drawn to making something out of nothing,
a habit since childhood. I'm so unreliable no one asks me, "What's
that?" knowing that a sandhill crane in a remote field can become a
yellow Volkswagen. In moments, the girl's blue dress becomes the
green I prefer. Words themselves can adopt confusing colors, which
can become a burden while reading. You don't have to become what
you already are, which is a relief. Today in Sierra Vista while carry-
ing six plastic bags of groceries I fell down. Can that be a curb? What
else? The ground rushed up and I looked at gravel inches away, a
knee and hands leaking blood. Time and pain are abstractions you
can't see but you know when they're with you like a cold hard wind.
It's time to peel my heart off my sleeve. It sits there red and glisten-
ing like a pig's heart on Grandpa's farm in 1947 and I have to some-
how get it back into my body.

Early Fishing

There was a terrible mistake when I checked my driver's license today and saw that I'd be seventy next week. At 3:30 AM I was only ten and heard Dad with that coal shovel on a cool May morning in the basement, his steps on the stairs, then he woke me for trout fishing with scrambled eggs, a little coffee in my milk, and then we were off in the car, a '47 Chevy two-tone, blue and beige, for the Pine River about an hour's distance up through Luther, the two-track off the county road muddy so he gunned it. He settled me near a deep hole in the bend of the river and then headed upstream to his favorite series of riffle corners. The water was a little muddy and streamer flies didn't work so I tied on a bright Colorado spinner and a gob of worms. In the next four hours I caught three good-sized suckers and three small brown trout. I kept the trout for our second breakfast and let the suckers go. It was slow enough that I felt lucky that I'd brought along a couple dozen Audubon cards to check out birds. Back then I wanted to see a yellow-bellied sapsucker and I still do. While I dozed I hooked my biggest brown trout, about two pounds, and wished I had been awake. When Dad came back downstream and started a small fire I fibbed about my heroism catching the trout, a lifelong habit. He fried the fish with bacon grease stored in a baby food jar. He cut up a quarter-loaf of Mother's Swedish rye bread and we ate the fish with the bread, salt and pepper. Dad napped and I walked back into the dense swampy woods getting a little lost until he called out after waking. Midafternoon we packed up to leave with a creel full of trout for the family and I left my fly rod in the grass behind the car and Dad backed over it. I had paid ten bucks for it earned at fifteen cents an hour at lawn and garden work. Dad said, "Get your head out of your ass, Jimmy." They're still saying that.

Mapman

I like to think that I was a member of the French Resistance though I was only three years old and lived on a farm in Northern Michigan when Germany invaded France, an unforgivable act but then the seams of history burst with the unforgivable. The mind itself is a hoax that feeds on its own fanciful stories. In Marseille the Germans cut off my feet at the ankle and left me for dead, as they say. I cauterized my stumps on the coals of a bonfire near the Vieux-Port and took several weeks to crawl over the hills past Cassis to Bandol. The German soldiers ignored me crawling along with my knees wrapped in burlap. In Bandol I was recognized as the Mapman by a vintner and was smuggled back to Marseille under the straw in a cartload of pigs. Pig shit repels prying noses. I was hidden behind a false wall in the basement and from my candlelit table spread with the maps of war I helped direct the routes of passage through the countryside for the Resistance. Intensely detailed maps of southern France were my wallpaper and improbably intimate to me. We lost thousands of brave men but saved thousands or so they said. Sandrine who worked at the bakery sent down nude photos of herself and I considered them maps of the mysteries of women. I grew fat on all the bread sent down to me with summer vegetables. I began to grow thin in November when a Nazi colonel set up a desk in the bakery to avoid the bitterness of the mistral and the employees had to be careful about the use of the dumbwaiter. Once in the middle of the night someone courageous sent down a case of simple red wine which I drank in two days to experience the glories and ample delusions of drunkenness. I even tried to dance to silence on my healed stumps, an unsuccessful venture. The logical question anyone might ask is how an American could be of any use to the Resistance? My father was an archaeologist from the University of Chicago and my mother was a French anthropologist. They spent the entirety of the 1920s and '30s in the south of France investigating the remnants of ancient cultures. This period of time included my childhood and youth and I was happy indeed to accompany them on their research wanderings. Both parents were executed in Aix-en-Provence in 1942 for hiding Jews in their rural home. My own obsessions from an early age were botany and cartography. I was a child "crazed with maps," as the poet Rimbaud would have it. My specialty in cartography was topography, the peculiarities of varying elevations. Many of us understand that along with geological upheavals the world has been shaped by the movement of water. Water is the primal signatory of earth shape. I certainly don't wish to overstate my importance to the underground. It finally wasn't that much because of human frailty and the lunar, impassive cruelty of the Gestapo. I was only the Mapman giving the latitudinal and longitudinal coordinates for relatively safe foot passage from place to place. Consider the deer. There are tens of thousands of them and they are rarely seen because they don't wish to be seen. Learn the traits of peasants and deer, was my advice. They do their best not to be shot. I was a Mercator genius of sorts having hiked the countryside for nearly twenty years and studied the terrain with the attention a farmer offers to his own land. Animal tracks are the safest route of passage on this earth. When liberation came I remained in the bakery basement. Why try to see the world when history had stolen my feet? I was helped upstairs on my stumps once a week and could see down a narrow street to a blue slice of the Mediterranean but had never acquired a particular interest in the sea so it was merely one of those banal Sunday paintings and other people were only marionettes who smelled oddly after my four years of solitary confinement. Finally an old shipwright and an army doctor carved me feet out of wood and leather. The shipwright spoke a peculiar Marseille patois that I didn't understand and that made him a good companion after war made one properly speechless. Unfortunately as I began to be up and around I found I could go nowhere in my former beloved landscapes that I had known since childhood. As with history the landscape became only the story of the dead, the invisible crosses of my compatriots obscenely obvious in my mapmaker's brain. I moved north to the Morvan about thirty kilometers from Autun to a small woodcutter's cottage where I was quite ignorant of the invisible graves in the landscape. Soon enough there will be no one left capable of reimagining my past, my story, and we will become the victims of books. I do have the fond memory of a goodbye picnic I had with a poet friend near L'Isle-sur-la-Sorgue. We stared down into a tiny rock pool in a creek, confident that it held no ghosts.

The *Penitentes*

It is hard not to see poets as *penitentes* flaying their brains for a line. They have imaginary tattoos that can't be removed. They think of themselves as mental Zorros riding the high country while far below moist and virginal señoritas wait impatiently in the valley. Poets run on rocks barefoot when shoes are available for a dime. They stand on cliffs but not too close to the fatal edge. They have examined their unfamiliar motives but still harvest the wildflowers they never planted. The horizon has long since disappeared behind them. They have this idea that they have been cremated but aren't quite dead. Their ashes are eyes. At night the stars sprinkle down upon them like salt. At noon they are under porches with the rest of the world's stray and mixed-breed dogs, only momentarily noticed, and are never petted except by children and fools.

Very Small Wars

There's no flash here among the troops. We just want to protect our freedom, well-being and safety. It occurred to me that if I were a vehicle I wouldn't be a Maserati but a John Deere or Farmall tractor, nothing special. Way out here in the country Linda runs a trapline and I patrol daily for rattlers though I can't find the one she saw in the garage behind her gardening tools. She kills a half-dozen mice a day but is now thinking of a device called "Mice Cube" which traps them alive so I could release them on a Republican's lawn when I drive to town for a drink. I'm squeamish about killing mice, once having tried to save one with a broken neck in the trap who looked up at me imploringly. I was drunk and actually sobbed, putting the little critter on a cotton bed in a matchbox. In the morning she was gone and probably eaten by our retarded cat Elie who sits under the bird feeder all day waiting for lunch to fall from the heavens. Also there's a sentimentality about murder as I intend to shoot Hungarian partridge, grouse, woodcock, maybe an antelope for the table this fall. Linda is rather matter-of-fact about killing mice but women are natural hunters. Rattlesnakes aren't innocent. One killed my dog Rose. Our little grandson Silas walks in the flower beds, which we pre-check for vipers. The mind tires of this war but my peace plan is faulty: let rattlers in the house to kill and eat the mice. The last rattler I shot was within a foot of the front door and struck at our old, deaf cat Warren. I blew the snake's head into oatmeal with my *pistola* in a surge of anger. I am a man of peace. Send suggestions. It's not known in Washington, D.C., but death is death.

Land Divers

On the TV screen it said, "Warning: Indigenous Nudity," which sets you up for what you saw in *National Geographic* as a kid in the forties. These natives have the smiles we haven't seen since we were children. They own a lot of pigs on this island, and raise taro, and have the ocean for fish. Their religion is real complicated like some of our own. It's a tough job to explain the meaning of life when you have no idea. They build towers of logs and poles and jump off them headfirst with a long vine tied to an ankle, just long enough to stop them short of the ground or else they'd dash out their brains. Is this to threaten inevitable death? It is to say, Yes I know I'll die, but right now I'm flying if only for a moment. I'm wondering when I watch this film, which nearly everyone has seen like the Budweiser Clydesdales, whether native peoples didn't take this ritual a step further. There was a primitive oceanic culture that believed that after death we're capable of swimming around under the ground and wherever we finally come up is the afterlife we deserve. Some bad people had to swim for years but if you were good it was a mere dunking and you would come up where you already were as a new grandchild. Should we believe this? Why not? Unfortunately the only mammal I know vaguely capable of this is the badger, always a lonely and irascible creature, who can bury himself in a minute and chew off a dog's leg in less time than that. A friend shot a badger in the head to make him turn loose a dog but in death the badger continued chewing. Meanwhile, up on a tower we poise for the jump hoping we're not so fat our vine-bound leg will pull off, unmindful that the gods favor ordinary blackbirds in this art.

Easter 2008

Death is liquid the scientists are saying. We'll enter the habitat of water after giving up the control we've never had. There will be music as when we used to hear a far-off motorboat while swimming underwater. Some of the information is confusing though water makes music simply being itself. Since we won't have ears and mouths it will be a relief to give up language, to sense a bird flying overhead without saying *bird* and not to have to hear our strenuous blood pumping this way and that. You don't need ears to hear the planets in transit, or the dead who have long since decided there is nothing more to say but *glory* in their being simply part of the universe held in the area of a thrall called home. When Christ rose from the water he wondered at seeing the gods he had left far behind when he finished his forty days in the wilderness.

Shortcomings

Only thirteen birds at first light. Some are near the French doors to tell me that they need more food. I did poorly at French and Italian but know how to ask for food in their countries. So did birds up north where chickadees would peck at the window saying the feeder is empty. Down here the different types of orioles say, "More grapes please." I know dog language fairly well but then dogs hold a little back from us because we don't know their secret names given them by the dog gods. Nature withholds and hides from us until we try to learn her languages. Yesterday a Chihahuan raven replied to me in a voice I had never heard before saying, "You don't speak very well." In 20,000 walks you're bound to learn a little. Doors finally open where you didn't know there were doors and windows lose their dirty glass. After a night of extreme pain I had glimpses of a new world. A rock brought me to red tears. Of course death will interrupt us soon enough, or so they say, but right now walking through a canyon I can't imagine not walking through a canyon. On a new side of night I asked the gods to not let me learn too much.

The World's Fastest White Woman

I saw this documentary about the fastest white woman in the world, ever so little behind a black woman by tenths of seconds in the 100 and 200 meters. Or at least I think I saw a documentary or perhaps my mind created this true-to-life story. She was running along the wonderful paths in the ravines in Toronto and you could see skyscrapers through the green leafy trees. In a ditzy TV interview she said that she easily outran a group of rapists in L.A. They wanted to shoot at her when they couldn't catch her but a wise rapist said that he had stopped the shooting under the accurate presumption that she would eventually run in a circle back to them due to the fact that one leg is always slightly shorter than the other and no one can run very far in a straight line. That's why tracks are always circular. I run in very tight circles due to a deformed left leg my parents couldn't afford to get fixed, another mark of Cain. I may as well put on track shoes and twirl. Anyway this fastest white woman in the world is both sad and angry that she can't run around the world because of the water problem. The oceans, whether in their placidity or torment, are not friendly to feet. Even Jesus while walking on the Sea of Galilee knew that sinking was a possibility. After I met her a single time briefly (she was running in place) in Toronto I introduced myself by letter as a famed physiologist curious about her speed. I bought a white smock and latex gloves and examined the juncture of her hips and thighs and buttocks that propelled her at such an alarming rate. Of course she was more muscular but I found nothing unlike the other eleven women in my life. We were in Austin at the University of Texas and after the minute examination we went down to the track and I tried to film her running but I couldn't figure out the cheap video camera I had bought at Costco. We then went to a BBQ shack where she ate a huge triple-portion brisket platter with the hottest of sauces and an ample bowl of pickled jalapeños. She was bereft by her inability to run around the world but somehow managed to eat saying that she needed 7,000 calories a day to maintain her weight of 119 pounds. It was then that I wiped away her tears with a blue paper napkin and suggested that we go to the North Pole where she could run around the world in seconds, but like many of the young she apparently didn't understand geography. We then went to my not-so-lavish hotel suite where she quickly ate the entire contents of the complimentary fruit bowl. During a long night of love in which we discovered that we didn't like each other I explained to her that her obsession was to beat a dead horse over and over until it became an actual dead horse in the brain, stinking and immovable. I had to be cautious in our lovemaking because her feet had callused spurs that reminded me of the female duckbill platypus that has poisonous spurs on her back feet that can kill a small dog. She wept and at dawn confessed that everyone in her family was morbidly obese and that her speed was never more than a second ahead of her prodigious appetite. I called room service for the dozen scrambled eggs, one-pound sausage patty, quart of OJ and seven pieces of toast she needed. I drank a pot of coffee and read a newspaper to see if the world deserved to exist. We drove into the country until we found a remote road where she ran in front of my Hertz. I admired the way she was staying a single step in front of her madness in the way that so many of us do by merely watching the clock where each tick brings us safely over the lip of the future, our madness a split second behind us.

My Leader

Now in the dog days of summer Sirius is making a dawn peek over the mountains, or so I think being fairly ignorant of stars. It's been over 90 degrees for thirty days and here in Montana the earth has begun to burn. I recall a hot late morning down in Veracruz in a poor-folks cemetery waiting for a restaurant to open so I could eat my lunch, a roasted robalo with lime and garlic, a beer, a nap and then to start life over again watching ships in the harbor that needed to be watched. The old cemetery keeper points out a goat in the far corner and shrugs, making hand and finger gestures to explain how the goat crawls over the stone fence or wriggles though the loose gates. I follow the goat here and there and he maintains what he thinks is a safe distance. He eats fresh flowers and chews plastic flowers letting them dribble in bits from his lips. A stray dog trots down a path and the goat charges, his big balls swinging freely. The dog runs howling, squeezing through a gate. The goat looks at me as if to say, "See what I have done." Now he saunters and finds fresh browse in the shade of the catafalque of the Dominguez family. I sit down in the shade and he sits down facing me about ten feet away, his coat mangy and his eyes quite red. I say, "I'm waiting for my roasted fish." He stares, only understanding Spanish. I say, "In this graveyard together we share the fatal illness, time." He stretches for a mouthful of yellow flowers quickly spitting them out. Baptists say the world is only 6,000 years old, but goats are fast learners. They know what's poisonous as they eat the world.

Cold Wind

I like those old movies where tires and wheels run backwards on horse-drawn carriages pursued by indians, or Model A's driven by thugs leaning out windows with tommy guns ablaze. Of late I feel a cold blue wind through my life and need to go backwards myself to the outback I once knew so well where there were too many mosquitoes, blackflies, curious bears, flowering berry trees of sugar plum and chokeberry, and where sodden and hot with salty sweat I'd slide into a cold river and drift along until I floated against a warm sandbar, thinking of driving again the gravel backroads of America at thirty-five miles per hour in order to see the ditches and gulleys, the birds in the fields, the mountains and rivers, the skies that hold our 10,000 generations of mothers in the clouds waiting for us to fall back into their arms again.

Burning the Ditches

Over between Dillon and Butte in the valley near Melrose they're burning out the ditches on a moist, sad morning when my simpleminded heart aches for another life. Why can't I make a living trout fishing? The same question I posed sixty years ago to my father. I got drunk last night, an act now limited to about twice a year. It was the olive-skinned barmaid Nicole who set me off as if the dead filaments of my hormones had begun to twitch and wiggle again. In the morning I walk a canyon two-track and hear a canyon wren for the first time outside Arizona. Up the mountainside I see the long slender lines of the billowing smoke from the ditch fires, confused because the wren song is drawing me south to my winter life on the Mexican border. The ditches get choked with vegetation and they burn them out in the spring so the irrigation water can flow freely. I suddenly determine that the smell of spring is the smell of the rushing river plus the billions of buds on trees and bushes. Back in the home ground, the Upper Peninsula of Michigan, when loggers went to town one day a month, they called getting drunk "burning out the grease." In 1958 a friend in San Francisco burned out his veins shooting up hot paregoric, a cheap high. It's safer for me to continue smoldering just below the temperature of actual flame wondering if there's a distant land where life freely flows like a river. Years ago in a high green pasture near timberline I watched a small black bear on its back rolling back and forth and shimmying to scratch its back, pawing the air with pleasure, not likely wanting to be anywhere or anyone else.

Alien

It was one of those mornings when my feet seemed unaware of each other and I walked slowly up a canyon wash to avoid tripping. It was warmish at dawn but the sun wouldn't quite come out, having missed a number of good chances, or so I thought studying the antic clouds that were behaving as sloppily as the government. I was looking for a wildflower, the penstemon, but stopped at a rock pool in a miniature marsh seeing a Mojave rattlesnake curled up in the cup of a low-slung boulder. Since this snake can kill a cow or horse I detoured through a dense thicket then glimpsed the small opening of a side canyon I had not noticed in my seventeen years of living down the road. How could I have missed it except that it's my habit to miss a great deal? And then the sun came out and frightened me as if I had stumbled onto a well-hidden house of the gods, roofless and only a hundred feet long, backed by a sheer wall of stone. I smelled the telltale urine of a mountain lion but no cave was visible until I looked up at a passing Mexican jay who shrieked the usual warning. We move from fear to fear. I knew the lion would be hiding there in the daytime more surely than I had seen the snake. They weren't guardians. This is where they lived. These small rock cathedrals are spread around the landscape in hundreds of variations but this one had the rawness of the unseen, giving me an edge of discomfort rarely felt in nature except in Ecuador and the Yucatán where I had appeared as a permanent stranger. I sat down with my back tight against a sheer wall thinking that the small cave entrance I faced by craning my neck must be the home of the old female lion seen around here not infrequently and that she could only enter from a crevasse at the top, downward into her cave. This is nature without us. This is someone's home where I don't belong.

Snake Woman

She moved like a snake if a snake had feet. I was sitting in a café when she passed on a narrow side street in Modena, Italy. Her head twitched on a thin neck, the tip of her pink tongue testing the air. Her feet were too far behind a body almost too slender to walk, and under her long skirt it was unlikely that there were actual legs. From a few blocks away near the military school the cadet band was playing our own Marine hymn for the Zampone Festival, which is stuffed pig's leg, but the rhythm of her walking was against the music. She must be a local fixture because no one else noticed her. I recall as a boy I found a tiny bird the size of a thumbnail but Mother said it was just a bumblebee so I fed it to a blacksnake that lived under our dock. Now fifty yards down the street the woman is definitely a snake, undulating upright, defying gravity on the way home to eat bugs and mice. I think of following her but I'm a little frightened. I once stepped on our blacksnake in my bare feet. I bet she crawls up her stairs. I wish I had never seen her.

Late

What pleasure there is in sitting up on the sofa late at night smoking cigarettes, having a small last drink and petting the dogs, reading Virgil's sublime *Georgics,* seeing a girl's bare bottom on TV that you will likely never see again in what they call real life, remembering all the details of when you were captured by the indians at age seven. They gave you time off for good behavior but never truly let you go back to your real world where cars go two ways on the same streets. The doctors will say it's bad for an old man to stay up late petting his lovely dogs. Meanwhile I look up from Virgil's farms of ancient Rome and see two women making love in a field of wildflowers. I'm not jealous of their real passion trapped as they are within a television set just as my doctors are trapped within their exhausting days and big incomes that have to be spent. Lighting a last cigarette and sipping my vodka I examine the faces of the sleeping dogs beside me, the improbable mystery of their existence, the short lives they live with an intensity unbearable to us. I have turned to them for their ancient language not my own, being quite willing to give up my language that so easily forgets the world outside itself.

Ninety-six-Year-Old Estonian

Just before World War II I was smuggled into America on a tramp freighter. There were a hundred of us and only one toilet on the stormy seas. We were never allowed up on deck during our entire passage. The dark was good practice for twenty-five days because a job had been arranged for me in a basement in Brooklyn, twelve hours a day seven days a week so that I didn't see America in the daylight for five months since I arrived in November. In fact I only saw daylight in the late spring, summer, and early fall for ten years. I was held there by fear, working for a Chinaman who had paid my passage. My job was stamping out rubber guns and knives for novelty stores. After a decade of this I strangled the Chinaman and stole his money and consequently had a happier life working on freighters between New York City and ports in Central and South America as a deckhand, taking extra shifts to get daylight hours. For a while I was a thief and gambler but quit this profitable life because it was night work. It was far better to work on vegetable farms in New Jersey, all in the wonderful daylight. Now that I can barely move I have this small room in my nephew's junky house in Nyack. I spend every day from dawn to dusk sitting in this chair watching the light off the Hudson River, which changes every second.

Vallejo

I keep thinking of César Vallejo's wine bottles, the moldy ones he picked up on the streets to return for *sous*. His girlfriend helped though on certain days it was slim pickings and they only shared a baguette sitting on a bench in the Montparnasse Cemetery, the location of his destiny, also one of the best places to watch birds in Paris what with all of those trees and upright stones to perch upon. A baguette is to eat with something else but if you have nothing else it will work for half an hour until it seems your stomach has begun to eat itself because it has. So many years after he died I still wanted him to go back to Peru before it was too late and settle for their 350 varieties of potatoes rather than die on a cold, rainy Thursday in Paris as he predicted he would. I started reading him fifty years ago and still do, seeing him write his poems in incomprehensible Paris, selling empty bottles, eating his bread, dying. He sailed off on a dream ship of food and full wine bottles. I don't want to keep thinking about César Vallejo as I sit on the sofa at midnight having just heard on television that everything in nature is disappearing. Someone is always trying to scare us. Everyone wants to be a hit man for God these days. Meanwhile it's the first week of May and I'm waiting for the curlews to arrive in the soon-to-be-flooded pasture across the road, also the tiniest of wildflowers only recently noticed in the spavined field to the south. I keep seeing the orioles, grosbeaks, warblers, lazuli buntings I left behind last week on the border wearing their clearly unimaginable colors as if they'll never disappear. Vallejo stands more revealed today. The gods loved him, dead or alive. They don't care if we're pissing blood or that our hearts strangle themselves to do their bidding.

Late Spring

Because of the late, cold wet spring the fruit of greenness is suddenly upon us so that in Montana you can throw yourself down just about anywhere on a green grassy bed, snooze on the riverbank and wake to a yellow-rumped warbler flittering close to your head then sipping a little standing water from a moose track. Of course pitching yourself downward you first look for hidden rocks. Nothing in nature is exactly suited to us. Meanwhile everywhere cows are napping from overeating, and their frolicsome calves don't remember anything except this bounty. And tonight the calves will stare at the full moon glistening off the mountain snow, both snow and moon white as their mother's milk. This year the moisture has made the peonies outside my studio so heavy with their beauty that they droop to the ground and I think of my early love, Emily Brontë. The cruelty of our different ages kept us apart. I tie and prop up the peonies to prolong their lives, just as I would have nursed Emily so she could see another spring.

Old Bird Boy

Birds know us as "the people of the feet." I am watched as I walk around and around my green studio, a man of many beaten paths. Near me a willow flycatcher arcs in its air dance to catch a grasshopper, a swift move that I compare to nothing whatsoever that I do. They own the air we breathe. I've studied the feet of the bridled titmouse for years, how they seem to be made of spiderwebs so precariously attached to perch or ground, also the feet of the golden eagle which are death angels, and then the wings of all birds which on close inspection don't seem possible. Most birds own the ancient clock of north and south, a clock that never had hands, the god-time with which the universe began. As the end draws nearer I've taken to praying to be reincarnated as a bird, and if not worthy of that, a tree in which they live so I could cradle them as I did our daughters and grandsons. Three times last April down on the border a dozen Chihuahuan ravens accompanied me on walks when I sang the right croaking song. I was finally within them. For the first time in my life I dared to say aloud, "I am blessed."

On Horseback in China

I followed this man across China for three months. I had a string of
five horses though two were daffy and didn't ride well in the west-
ern mountains except with my interpreter in the saddle. She was less
than four feet and weighed but fifty pounds at most. She said that
her name meant Jane in Chinese and she had studied at Oxford for
three free years because the Englishmen decided not to notice her.
She had a tiny dog that lived in the sleeve of her robe. The horses
were fond of this little dog as they often are of barn cats. My inter-
preter's dog ate a mere three thimblefuls of pork broth every day
and unlike other dogs was without curiosity for our eclectic meals of
yellow snake, monkey udders, a stew of duck rectums. Our journey
began on the mainland near Hong Kong appropriately enough on
April Fool's Day and ended on July 4, and when I dropped a string
of firecrackers from a fiftieth-floor window I prayed they didn't land
in a baby carriage. Hotel windows don't open anymore but I keep a
glass cutter in my checked luggage with which I carve a tiny open-
ing to relieve my claustrophobia. The trip itself was exhausting and
to a degree hastened my aging, plus I depleted a goodly portion of
my life's savings in my attempt to trace a man who didn't want to be
traced except in the 2,400 messages he left here and there, encoded
in poems. My route was circular and at no time could I give up or I
would lose the exorbitant deposit on the horses. A low point was at
the former hunting lodge of the famed Prince of Nine Gongs (T'ang
dynasty) where I became ill from a soup made of the rumen of yak
bellies smuggled in from the Arctic Circle of Alaska by a diplomat.
After three days of purging I resolved to eat only rice, an impossi-
ble program except for those who wish to die, as Jane pointed out.
The landscape and my thoughts dissolved into each other, becom-
ing liquid, and I recalled a line from a poet I disliked, "You are only
where you are minus you." In honor of our liquidity we become the

landscape down to the horse beneath us. One evening in the mountains camped by a waterfall I heard the screaming of monkeys and then the roar of a tiger at which point the monkeys fell silent. My motive for the trip? To discover if we are only the varying sums of our everyday lives. Up until this trip to China I had no clear understanding of my past and certainly no interest in seeing into the future. A decisive moment of satori came when a giant black mastiff that had been guarding a nearby herd of sheep entered the circle of light cast by our campfire and swallowed Jane's teeny dog in a single impulsive gulp that resembled a reverse burp. Jane wept piteously, flopping around like a freshly caught fish on the bottom of a wooden boat. I tried to console her but she explained that the dog was actually her soul. Later that day one of our horses got loose, swam through the rapids of a vast river and on the other side looked back for a moment in farewell before escaping into the green foothills of distant mountains. One day camped by a small lake it occurred to me that the fish we were eating were essentially the same fish eaten by Jesus and the Buddha. I was alarmed by the idea that the contents of life are indeed limited. That evening Jane told me that she was seventy years old after we collected an encrypted message in a despondent village that had lost its mayor when his wife stabbed him on learning of his affair with a retarded girl. This could have happened anywhere in the world. As time passed, as it will, I was becoming generally less mournful and after spending the night at a farm I apologized to a mother pig for eating a piglet of hers the night before but she pardoned me saying that she had eaten a human child when she escaped into the forest as a wild young girl-pig. I began to enjoy my lack of direction after I lost our compass at the beginning of the third month. Confusion ensued because Jane was useless over her lost soul and spent much of her time wrapped in her child's red sleeping bag. My gestures at a Chinese version of a department store were misunderstood and we were directed to the mountain dwelling of the hermit rather than a place to purchase a compass. At the store they seemed amused at the business card my interpreter had devised for me giving my name as Lord Zero. My travels had been eased by my semidiplomatic passport arranged by a friend, a U.S. congressman famed in China for removing trade barriers. Of course world trade is more important than marriage or religion. In any event we arrived after three days' ride into the mountains and the hermit immediately restored Jane's soul by serving her a boiled potato. He said that everything is to be found in the ordinary. It was then that it occurred to me that without travel we can't understand the madness of travel. This separates us slightly from the brief journey of the potato. I certainly lack courage and am no man's hero except to my children when they were young. My only peculiarity is swimming rivers alone at night. However, all my life I've seemed to love what our British cousins call the "edgelands," those grand pieces of land without economic value of any consequence. This is even more so in China where the press of more than a billion souls covers land of value as a swarm of honeybees collected around their queen. After riding two thousand miles I was no less a fool when I returned home. Since I was absolutely witless with the language Jane was my mind and I was merely antennae for my future memories which arrived in moments. I ate my meals, rode a horse, studied the landscape, all too often forgetting why I had made the journey. For better or much worse the hands on the reins were my own. One night I slept with a peasant woman who tasted like a tart green apple sprinkled with salt. In the morning she made me a soup of rice, chicken's feet, garlic, green onions and hot peppers. My feet were bare and the resemblance between my feet and chicken's feet was apparent. A dog I called Black Muzzle in honor of a dog who lived a thousand years ago shared the soup. It is possible in life to feel fairly good about nothing in particular. The only conclusions I can offer are the obvious biological ones. I've always had the modest embarrassment of a nearly size 10 head and when I arrived at our home my little grandson Johnny was kneading pasta dough on our kitchen table. He asked, "Grandpa, your head is big, what's in it?" I said, "On this day nothing in particular."

A Strange Poem

The birds and beard turn gray.
You twist from the hips
and the black door is closer.
The neighbor's baby goes to college
and two pet dogs have their graves
hallowed by a bed of varied flowers.
You play with their toys in the yard
and eat from their sparkling bowls.
The woman you loved killed you
with her ass as a scorpion does.
At sea you die from drinking the water.
It took so many years to build this blood
that leaks out on the straw in Grandpa's barn.
The simpleminded mirror can't find me.
Like everyone else I took myself for granted.
Still I praised god who spawned me
from one of a billion hopeless eggs
in this river of air. I tried to run away
with the girl who stayed behind
like everyone else. Here on the lip of earth
the air is as fresh as the cyclamen the color of blood.
Back at my beloved dog bowl I bow
to the gods who gave me this life,
my fins, the water.

New World

This moment says no to the next.
Now is quite enough for the gathering birds
in the tall willows above the irrigation ditch.
It's autumn and their intentions are in their blood.
Looking up at these chattering birds I become dizzy,
but statistics say old men fall down a lot.
The earth is fairly soft here, so far from the world
of cement where people must live to make a living.
Despite the New Covenant you can't eat the field's lilies.
Today I think I see a new cold wind rushing through the air.
Of course I stare up too long because I love cedar waxwings,
their nasalate click and hiss, their cantankerous joy.
I fall and the dogs come running. Mary licks my face.
I tell them that this is a world where falling is best.

Barking

The moon comes up.
The moon goes down.
This is to inform you
that I didn't die young.
Age swept past me
but I caught up.
Spring has begun here and each day
brings new birds up from Mexico.
Yesterday I got a call from the outside
world but I said no in thunder.
I was a dog on a short chain
and now there's no chain.

René Char

In the morning when the tilt of the world
is just so
the sunlight races down the small mountain
facing our porch
so fast you couldn't possibly
beat it in track shoes
nor would you want to try. It's too steep
and the rock is crumbly.
Once in Three R Canyon I saw a mountain
lion a half mile
distant flow up such a rock face and suddenly
was struck by my fleshy
limitations. I read that some women run with wolves
but I walk with opossums
and someday will slow to the desert tortoise's
stately pace.
Char says that a poet has only to be there when the bread
comes fresh from the oven.

Peonies

The peonies, too heavy with their beauty,
slump to the ground. I had hoped
they would live forever but ever so slowly
day by day they're becoming the soil of their birth
with a faint tang of deliquescence around them.
Next June they'll somehow remember to come alive again,
a little trick we have or have not learned.

Good Friday

Release yourself. Life is a shock to the system.
It was to the small javelina ever flattening
on the yellow line on a hot afternoon.
Release yourself. You've always doubted cars,
remembering when trains and horses were enough
and boats kept our ocean skies unmarred.
Release yourself. Your doubt is only the patina
of shit the culture paints on those in the margins.
Tomorrow the full moon is on Good Friday,
the blind face of the gods who can't see us anymore.

Insight

After we die we hover for a while
at treetop level with the mourners
beneath us, but we are not separate
from them nor they from us.
They are singing but the words
don't mean anything in our new language.

The Home

If my body is my home
what is this house full of blood
within my skin? I can't leave it
for a moment but finally will. It knows
up and down, sideways, the texture
of the future and remnants of the past.
It accepts moods as law no matter
how furtively they slip in and out
of consciousness. It accepts dreams as law
of a different sort as if they came from
a body well hidden within his own.
He says, "Pull yourself together," but he
already is. An old voice says, "Stay close to home."

Old Times

When I revived at dawn I didn't know
where I had been in the manner that occasionally life
imitates the childishness of science fiction.
The local mountains had become immense stupas
and there was a long band of fire in the east.
I bounded along in silly fifty-foot strides
unable to identify the huge orange birds that became
that color from flying low through the fire.
What am I to make of this? Where did it come
from to the weary human who'd rather parse
the mysteries of oatmeal topped with strawberries,
but then any kid knows that during a long night
the imagination thumbs its nose at civilization
as the lid of a jar screwed on too tight
that has no idea what its true contents are.
The billions of neurons fed by a couple of trillion
cells aren't confused. Perhaps a simpleminded
neuron remembers when the mountains were stupas
where small gods lived and 500-pound
birds fled from grass fires on the vast savannas
and man's ancestors wore seven-league boots
getting places either quickly or slowly without clocks.

Midnight Blues Planet

We're marine organisms at the bottom of the ocean
of air. Everywhere esteemed nullities rule our days.
How ineluctably we travel from our preembryonic
state to so much dead meat on the ocean's hard floor.
There is this song of ice in our hearts. Here we struggle
mightily to keep our breathing holes opened
from the lid of suffocation. We have misunderstood the stars.
Clocks make our lives a slow-motion frenzy. We can't get
off the screen back into the world where we could live.
Every so often we hear the current of night music
from the gods who swim and fly as we once did.

Complaint & Plea

Of late I've been afflicted by too many hummingbirds,
a red moon rising again in the smoke of forest fires,
a record long heat tsunami, the unpardonable vigor
of the hollyhocks pressing against the green studio,
their gorgeous trashiness as flowers (some call
them weeds), the fledgling redtail hawks crying
all day because they don't want to fly, the big rattler
I shot near our front door twisting itself into
the usual question mark, the river I want to fish
turbulent and brown from a distant thunderstorm,
the studio steps I fell off with the ground I used
to love floating up to meet me, the deepest sense
that life which is a prolonged funeral service
won't behave, that I'm living within a glass orb
that a monster brat won't stop shaking. A friend
wrote, "I have moments when I think life
may have gotten to be too much for me or that
I haven't gotten to be enough for it." Yes, life
is a holographic merry-go-round that whirls
at the speed of light in all directions at once.
To whom may I address my plea that the river
clear so that I might go fishing? The fish
must learn that pretty flies can have hooks in them.

Friends

Dogs, departed companions,
I told you that the sky would fall in
and it did. How will we see each other again
when we're without eyes? We'll figure it out
as we used to when you led me back
to the cabin in the forest in the dark.

Small Gods

My hope is that this minuscule prayer
will reach out to the god unknown I just sensed
passing in the rivulet of breeze above the mere rivulet
of water in this small arroyo. To the skittering insect
this place is as large as the Sea of Galilee.
In prayer I'm a complicated insect, moving
this way and that. The insect before me puzzles
over its current god, my dog Zilpha, who watches
with furrowed brow and thinks, "Should I paw
at this bug in this shallow pool, bite it, roll
on it in this tiny creek in the late afternoon heat,
or perhaps take another nap?" She looks at her god,
which is me, understanding as her eyes close
that the gods make up their minds as they go.
They are as patient as the water in which they live,
and won't be surprised when they reach the sea
with their vast collection of reflections, the man, the dog,
the stars and moon and clouds, the javelina and countless
birds, bugs and minnows, the delicate sips of rattlers,
the boughs of mesquite, the carapace of the desert tortoise,
the heron footprints, the water's memories of earth.

Goat Boy

I no longer lead my life. I'm led.
The sexuality of insects tells us that intentional
life is a hoax but the gods tell us
that we are also gods. The sun kindly rises
on the snoring goat out by the barn.
He'll only do what he wants to do.
He eats potato peels and stares at the rising moon.
I believe in my calling like he believes in the moon.
How else could I see clearly at night?
We are nature, too, and some of us do less well
in this invented world, or if we do well for a while
there is that backward stare from these overplowed fields
to the wild woodlot and creek in the distance.
At seven I went out to play and was lost in the woods
for a day and never understood the way back home.

Night Weather

I was thinking that weather might be the reason
the phases of night can be laminated with melancholy
so that we sit tightly against our Formica desks
with tears arising as we plan our own funerals.
Verdi's *Requiem* won't play well in Montana
just as "A Mighty Fortress Is Our God" doesn't work in Paris.
If it's Arizona you can't sing "Shall We Gather at the River."
Funerals fade abruptly in this desert night when rain begins to fall
and I see the future blooming of April's penstemon and primrose,
and bird hatchlings much smaller than a marble,
hearts beating as they break the shells that still contain us
or if the shell's not there we still can't quite leave.

Up

Here I am at the gateless gate again hoping
to see father, mother, sister, brother.
Where did they come from? Where did they go?
I keep climbing this tree as old as the world
and have lost my voice up here in the thin air.

Time

Time our subtle poison runs toward us,
and through us, and out the other side.
We've never been in the future except for a moment.
Time's poison is in the air we breathe
and the faint taste in the water we drink.
We are dogs who love their morning walks
but not their names. They don't know they're dogs,
but no one had the right to give them the wrong names.
Time never told us to have faith in the sepulcher
that awaits us. The night carves us into separate acts,
but I do have faith in that turbulent creek
of blood within me.

Father

The old man's angleworm stares
at the ground where it was born.

He remembers his red wagon speeding
down the steep sidewalk and tipping over.

He followed the girl up the ladder
to the haymow, his face hot as the sun.

Sailing from the north into his alien homeland
he put his bony shoulder against the human glacier.

He failed to find a new bird species or the nymph
with golden snakes in her raven hair.

He aimed so high that his cousin clouds were ice.
Below, the green carapace of earth, the backs of birds.

He dug a hole in the woods for a perfect hiding place,
and when he finally emerged he was a book.

He reminded himself daily that he lived
in a world of elephants, dandelions, butterflies.

Now walking the thin, sharp edge of the grave
he thinks of oceans and birds, a missing brother.

The girl across the subway tracks in 1957 is still there
amid brackish ozone, boarding the train.

Eleven Dawns with Su Tung-p'o

1

On my seventieth birthday reading Su Tung-p'o
in the predawn dark waiting for the first birdcall.
"I'm a tired horse unharnessed at last," he said.
Our leaders say "connect the dots" but the dots
are the 10,000 visible stars above me.

2

Morning. Twenty-five degrees. Heavy frost descending
at 6:30 AM. The only sound the whisper
of green hackberry leaves falling,
a deep green carpet under each tree.
First bird, a canyon wren.
Sky azure, sun-gold mountain.
My ears not frozen shut,
my one eye open
to this morning in a cold world.

3

At dawn my mind chattered like
seven schoolgirls,
seven pissed-off finches at the feeder,
seven ravens chasing the gray hawk.
How to calm it down? Let the creek
run through it from ear to ear.

4

You can't expect anything.
Even dawn is a presumption.
More raptors this year after two
good monsoons. I found a lush
and hidden valley I couldn't bear
to enter today. It frightened me
as if it might be home to new species
of creatures God had forgotten to invent.
The old man is also a timid boy.

5

On solstice dawn I'm an old brat
lifting a hundred mental bandages.
Mt. Everest is covered with climbers' junk
and a golf club was left behind on the moon,
the East suffocates in malice and the West
in pink cotton candy. Sixty years ago
my brother told me that the rain was angel piss
and that turtles might kill me when I swam.
The solstice says "everything on earth is True."

6

Waiting for the light. I stand by her door
listening for breath. We've had 18,000 nights
but one of us will go first. The big moon
speaks to me with the silence
of a sleeping dog. First bird, the canyon wren.
I hear her say to her dog Mary, "Move over."

7

Press the coffee button, December 24, with the moon
the bright eyeball of a god. For a couple of
million years people were outside
and now they're mostly inside. Had Su Tung-p'o
heard of Jesus from the trade routes exchanging
gunpowder and pasta? He knew the true wilderness
is the soul which doesn't wear
the old shoes of time and space.

8

I felt ignored waking up in the cold dark
and planned a parade for myself leading
the dogs, Mary and Zilpha, down the creek bed.
I wield my walking stick like a drum major
pointing out the earth and sky to the earth and sky.
The dogs like javelina tracks but cringe at the paw prints
of the mountain lion. Five ravens sound the alarm.
I never was the lord of all I survey.

9

Late in life I've lost my country.
Everywhere there is the malice of unearned
power, top to bottom, bottom to top,
nearly solid scum. Very few can read or write.
Lucky for me we winter in this bamboo thicket
near a creek with three barrels of bird food.
With first light things seem a little better.

10

Don't probe your brain's sore tooth in the dark.
Let your mind drift to the mountains
where migrants are doubtless freezing
on the coldest night of the year. The dogs
found a nest beneath the roots of a big sycamore
tipped over in July's flood. The ashes of a tiny fire,
an empty water bottle, a pop-top can of beans
scorched by the coals. These dangerous people
whom we're being taught to hate like the Arabs.

11

I can't find the beginning, middle and end in the dark.
Will a kindly lightbulb help? Su Tung-p'o is dead
but I keep talking to him as I do my father
gone now these fifty years. I have no moves
left except to feed the birds at first light.
I have nearly lived out my exile, the statistics
say. Who knows what glorious wine comes next
in my sunny kingdoms of dogs, birds and fish?

The Quarter

Maybe the problem is that I got involved with the wrong crowd of gods when I was seven. At first they weren't harmful and only showed themselves as fish, birds, especially herons and loons, turtles, a bobcat and a small bear, but not deer and rabbits who only offered themselves as food. And maybe I spent too much time inside the water of lakes and rivers. Underwater seemed like the safest church I could go to. And sleeping outside that young might have seeped too much dark into my brain and bones. It was not for me to ever recover. The other day I found a quarter in the driveway I lost at the Mecosta County Fair in 1947 and missed out on five rides including the Ferris wheel and the Tilt-A-Whirl. I sat in anger for hours in the bull barn mourning my lost quarter on which the entire tragic history of earth is written. I looked up into the holes of the bulls' massive noses and at the brass rings puncturing their noses which allowed them to be led. It would have been an easier life if I had allowed a ring in my nose, but so many years later I still find the spore of the gods here and there but never in the vicinity of quarters.

About the Author

Jim Harrison, one of America's most versatile and celebrated writers, is the author of thirty books of poetry, fiction, and nonfiction–including *Legends of the Fall,* the acclaimed trilogy of novellas, and *The Shape of the Journey: New and Collected Poems.* His books have been translated into two dozen languages, and in 2007 he was elected to the American Academy of Arts and Letters. With a fondness for open space and anonymous thickets, he divides his time between Montana and southern Arizona.

The Chinese character for poetry is made up of two parts: "word" and "temple." It also serves as pressmark for Copper Canyon Press.

Since 1972, Copper Canyon Press has fostered the work of emerging, established, and world-renowned poets for an expanding audience. The Press thrives with the generous patronage of readers, writers, booksellers, librarians, teachers, students, and funders — everyone who shares the belief that poetry is vital to language and living.

Major funding has been provided by:

Anonymous
Beroz Ferrell & The Point, LLC
Cynthia Hartwig and Tom Booster
Lannan Foundation
National Endowment for the Arts
Cynthia Lovelace Sears and Frank Buxton
Washington State Arts Commission

Copper Canyon Press gratefully acknowledges the following individuals for their generous support of this publication:

Anonymous
Bruce S. Kahn
Peter Lewis and Johnna Turiano
Gregg Orr
Beef Torrey

For information and catalogs:

COPPER CANYON PRESS
Post Office Box 271
Port Townsend, Washington 98368
360-385-4925
www.coppercanyonpress.org

This book is set in Dante, a font that echoes the fifteenth-century type of Francesco Griffo. Dante was designed in 1954 by Giovanni Mardersteig. Over the years it has been reworked by Monotype for machine and digital composition. The book title is set in Mendoza, a typeface designed by José Mendoza y Almeida. Book design and composition by Valerie Brewster, Scribe Typography. Printed on archival-quality paper at McNaughton & Gunn.